For Daddy

Charles Graham Sampson

May 29, 1950 – February 19, 2024

You were more than a father.

You were my protector, my teacher, my steady ground.

Even in death, you found ways to remind me that love doesn't end

—it simply changes form.

Through feathers, black birds, coins, dreams, and whispers,

you've shown me again and again that you're still near.

This book is for you, and because of you.

Every word is a thank-you.

Every sign is a memory.

Every page is proof that spirit lives on.

"Those we love don't go away,

they walk beside us every day...

unseen, unheard, but always near,

still loved, still missed, and very dear."

— Author Unknown

Foreword

When someone we love passes, we are left with more than sorrow—we are left with questions, silence, and an ache that never quite fades. But sometimes, in that silence, something extraordinary happens. We begin to hear... signs.

Signs from the Spirit is more than a memoir. It's a bridge between two worlds. In these pages, Sondra Sampson opens her heart to share the sacred journey she experienced after the loss of her beloved father, Charles Graham Sampson. Through dreams, feathers, birds, numbers, whispers, and quiet moments, she came to understand what many feel but few speak aloud: the ones we've lost are not gone. They are transformed.

This book is both a tribute and an invitation—to believe in the unseen, to embrace healing, and to trust that spirit finds its way back to us. With honesty, warmth, and courage, Sondra shows that grief doesn't have to be the end of the story. It can be the beginning of a new kind of connection.

Whether you are grieving, searching, or simply open to the idea that love transcends death, *Signs from the Spirit* offers gentle guidance and powerful affirmation: You are not alone. The signs are there.

You just have to believe.

Preface

I didn't set out to write a book. I set out to survive grief. After my father, Charles

Graham Sampson, passed away, I found myself searching—for
meaning, for comfort, for *him.* What I didn't expect were the signs. They came softly
first: a black bird, a coin, a flickering light. And then more boldly—in dreams, in
songs,
in moments that caught my breath.
These weren't coincidences. They were conversations.

Writing these stories helped me heal, one memory at a time. It became a way to
honor
my father, to carry him with me, and to prove to myself that love doesn't die—it
just
changes form.

This book isn't polished with perfection. It's raw, real, and filled with heart. I wrote

it
for me. But I'm sharing it for *you*—for anyone who has lost someone and wondered
they're still near.

If you've ever whispered, "I miss you," to an empty room...

If you've ever cried at a song that came on *right when you needed it...*

If you've ever looked at the sky and asked for a sign...

Then this book was meant to find you.

Acknowledgments

First and foremost, I want to thank God for walking with me through the storm of grief and turning my pain into purpose. Without faith, I would not have recognized the signs or found the strength to share them.

To my Daddy, **Charles Graham Sampson**—thank you for loving me so deeply in life and continuing to show up in spirit. Every word in this book carries your heartbeat. I miss you endlessly, but I feel you always.

To my five beautiful children—**Ashley, Austin, Alyssa, Abby, and Ashton**—you are my light. Your love and encouragement remind me daily to keep going. Thank you for letting me pause, cry, write, and believe in something greater than what we see.

To my husband—thank you for standing beside me, for understanding my tears, and for never doubting this journey. Your quiet strength has helped hold me steady.

To my **mother Lorraine Douglas Sampson**, whose love runs deep and strong—you gave me the roots I needed to survive the hardest seasons. And to my **sister Tammie Sampson Goff**, thank you for walking this path of grief with me. We lost the same man, but in different ways. Your presence has helped me feel less alone.

To my ancestors and the **Lumbee Tribe**—I carry your stories, your resilience, and your sacred wisdom with every step. This book is also yours.

To the readers who pick up this book in moments of sorrow or searching—thank you. I hope these pages meet you with comfort, connection, and confirmation that your loved ones are still near.

And finally, to everyone who has shared their own signs with me along the way—your stories remind me that spirit is everywhere, and that healing becomes sacred when we speak it out loud.

Prologue

When the World Went Quiet

Grief doesn't knock. It doesn't ask permission.

It arrived for me the moment my father took his last breath. The world around me didn't explode—it went quiet. Too quiet. It was as if the trees paused, the wind forgot to blow, and time held its breath.

But that silence wasn't empty. It was the beginning of something sacred.

In the days that followed, I began to feel him—see him—in ways that defied logic but filled my soul. A black bird on the mailbox. A coin resting on his headstone. A song on the radio at just the right time. These weren't coincidences. They were signs. Clear, loving messages that death is not the end.

As a proud Lumbee woman, I was raised to believe in spirit, in ancestors, in the sacred rhythm of nature. But I didn't expect how deeply those teachings would come to life after my father passed. What began as small wonders became a full conversation between this world and the next.

This book is a record of that conversation.

Every chapter you'll read is a true moment—sometimes ordinary, sometimes otherworldly—where the spirit of my father broke through the veil to remind me:

Love doesn't die. It transforms.

These signs are not just mine. They are messages meant to be shared—with anyone who has lost someone and needed proof they're still near. You are not alone. And neither am I.

This is our story.

This is *Signs from the Spirit.*

Introduction

Learning to Listen Beyond the Veil

Grief changes everything. It rearranges your heart, your thoughts, and the way you see the world. But for me, it also opened a doorway—one I never expected.

When my father passed away, I didn't just lose a parent. I lost my protector, my storyteller, my steady hand in uncertain times. The silence that followed felt unbearable. I didn't know how to move forward without his voice, his advice, his laugh that could shake the room.

But then... the signs began.

At first, they were subtle. A black bird sitting on the mailbox. A coin placed mysteriously on his grave. A flicker of light at just the right moment. These small events felt like whispers in the dark—and when I paused long enough to really feel them, I knew they were messages from him.

This book is not about proving anything. It's not about religion, or superstition, or trying to convince anyone what's real.

It's about sharing.

Sharing the ways my father continued to speak to me after he crossed over. Sharing the comfort I found in feathers, butterflies, dreams, and soft breezes that seemed to carry his presence. Sharing the truth that connection never truly ends—it simply shifts forms.

Each chapter in this book reflects a different sign or experience that brought me closer to healing. Some will speak directly to your heart. Others may remind you of your own loved ones lost. But all are written with the hope that you'll begin to see the world around you with fresh eyes—watching for signs, for patterns, for messages wrapped in everyday moments.

Because when you start looking, listening, and believing, you'll realize the people you miss most...

never really left at all.

Chapter One

The First Sign

The evening after my father passed, the air felt unusually still—as if the world was holding its breath. I walked outside with my tea in hand, uncertain what to expect from the day. My heart was still broken, my body moving through the motions of grief. That's when I saw it: a single black bird perched on the mailbox, staring at me.

It didn't move. It didn't flinch. It just watched. I froze in place.

For a moment, I wondered if I imagined it. But the bird was real—and somehow, so was the feeling that flooded over me. Calm. Connection. Presence. As if Daddy was there, just beyond the veil, sending me a sign.

Growing up Lumbee, I'd always heard stories passed down about spirit messengers.

The old ones said black birds carried messages from the spirit world. I never took those words lightly, but I didn't fully understand them either—until that moment.

The bird tilted its head, and I swear, I could hear my daddy's voice in my memory:

"I'll always find a way to let you know I'm near."

Tears fell, but they weren't just from sadness. They came from something deeper—recognition. That was the first sign. And it was only the beginning.

Poem – A Feather at Dawn

A single black wing on my windowsill,

Morning hush, the world stood still.

Eyes that glowed, not made of fear—

I felt your soul was hovering near.

The coffee steam, the breath I took,

Turned pages back, like in a book.

You found me, Dad, across the line—

Your love remains, your spirit shines

Diary Entry

March 14

I didn't expect anything special today, but that bird on the mailbox changed everything. It wasn't random. I know it. The way it looked at me—bold, steady. Not afraid. Just... waiting. Like he wanted me to *see*.

It makes me believe more than ever that Daddy's really watching over me. Maybe I'm not crazy. Maybe signs are real. I feel him. I miss him. But I'm not alone.

Chapter Two

The Coins on the Tombstone

A week after Daddy's funeral, I visited his grave again, this time with no expectations. I only brought silence, my breath, and a small bouquet. As I approached, I saw something strange on the tombstone—three pennies and a dime, stacked neatly.

I didn't place them there.

There was no one else around. No wind. No reason.

I froze, my hand covering my mouth. In Lumbee tradition and across many Native stories, coins left on graves carry meaning. They symbolize visits, messages, or prayers paid forward. The number of coins? I'd learn later they matched the number of people who had been dreaming about Daddy that week—including me.

One of the pennies had the year I was born. Another had the year my father was drafted. The dime had the year I got married. Random? I think not.

I whispered, "Thank you, Daddy. I know it's you."

Poem – Copper and Memory

Coins don't speak, but they shine in the light,

A silent signal, a soul taking flight.

Pennies for thoughts that never will fade,

Dimes for the paths that your hands helped me pave.

Resting on stone, no sound, just grace,

A message from you in that sacred place.

Though I weep and walk away slow,

I feel your love in the things that glow.

Diary Entry

March 22

It's like he's finding ways to prove he's still around. I never told anyone, but I dreamed of Daddy last night again—he was younger, smiling like he used to after fixing the car. That same day, I found the coins.

I don't believe in coincidences anymore. I believe in signs.

Chapter Three

The Light in the Hallway

It was around midnight when the light flickered.

Our hallway light has never done that. It's not old. No storm. No power surge. Just a steady flicker for about 15 seconds, then it stopped. Just like that. But the strange thing? The flicker came right after I said, out loud, "Daddy, I miss you tonight."

I felt something shift in the air.

I walked toward the hallway slowly, goosebumps all over. Then the light blinked once more—as if to answer. Not in a scary way. It felt warm. Comforting. A soft presence. I looked up, smiled, and said, "I love you too."

That light never flickered again after that night.

Poem – Flicker of Love

One blink, two blinks—then silence returns,

A whisper of light where memory burns.

No bulb can explain what the heart understands,

That flicker was you, just brushing my hands.

So I stood in the glow and didn't feel fear,

Just a father's love gently drawing me near.

Even in silence, the signs still shine—

You speak in pulses, like rhythm divine.

Diary Entry

April 2

The hallway light flickered last night after I said I missed him. It wasn't electrical—I felt it in my gut. The energy changed. That's how I know it wasn't random. The way the air felt. Like a blanket laid softly over the room.

I think that's his way of answering me now—through light. Through feeling. Through warmth.

Chapter Four

The Dream Visit

I was walking along a wooded path in my dream—tall trees, sunlight streaking through the leaves, and everything so quiet it felt holy. Then I saw him.

Daddy.

He was standing at the edge of the trees, smiling in that way he did when he wanted me to know everything would be alright. He didn't speak. He didn't need to. He just opened his arms.

I ran to him and felt the hug—warm, strong, just like before. The scent of motor oil and fresh-cut grass clung to his flannel shirt. We stood there, father and daughter, in silence, holding what time had taken.

Then he whispered, "You're going to be okay. I've never left."

I woke up crying, but for the first time, I didn't feel alone. That wasn't a dream. That was a visit.

Poem – Between the Pines

In dreams you walk, so clear, so near,

Through pine and sun, you reappear.

No words are needed when hearts still know,

Where spirits meet and feelings grow.

Your flannel shirt, your weathered hand,

Still guides me gently through this land.

In dream's embrace, I found my peace—

Proof that love will never cease.

Diary Entry

April 8

Last night, I saw him again in my sleep. It wasn't a dream—it was different. It was real. The way I felt his arms, the smell of him. He *told* me I'd be okay. And I believe him. That comfort didn't come from inside me—it came from *him.*

I think heaven lets them visit us when we need it most.

Chapter Five

The Feather on the Windshield

It had been a tough day. I was frustrated, tired, and missing him more than usual. I asked aloud in the car, "Daddy, I just need a sign. Anything."

I turned the ignition off and sat there in silence.

Then I noticed it—a single white feather, drifting slowly down from the sky. It didn't blow away. It landed gently, perfectly, in the center of my windshield.

No birds around. No tree above me. Just blue sky.

I stared, stunned. Then I smiled through tears.

Feathers have always been sacred. Carriers of prayers. Gifts from the other side. That one wasn't random—it was Daddy saying, "I heard you."

Poem – A Feather Falls

One feather fell, no bird in flight,

Just sky above and morning light.

It found my car, my heart, my view—

A quiet sign that love shines through.

So weightless, soft, yet bold and true,

It whispered softly, "I'm near to you."

Though worlds apart, we're never gone—

You send me signs to carry on.

Diary Entry

April 14

The feather was the softest thing I've ever seen. And the way it landed—like it knew exactly where I'd be. I've always heard feathers mean angels are near. I believe it now. Daddy, I know you sent that to remind me I'm not alone. Thank you.

Chapter Six

The Radio That Turned On

It was early evening and the house was quiet. I hadn't touched the radio in days—it sat on the kitchen shelf collecting dust. I was in the middle of chopping vegetables when I heard it click on.

The volume rose gently, not sudden or jarring. Just... there. A soft hum of static, then a song began to play:

"You Are My Sunshine."

Daddy used to hum that when I was little—especially when I was scared of thunderstorms. It was *our song.*

I stood frozen, knife in hand, eyes filling with tears. The radio had no timer. No reason. No explanation. But the message was clear.

He found a way to sing to me again.

Poem – Sunshine in Static

No hand touched the dial, yet music came through,

A whisper, a hum, a song I once knew.

The notes floated out with memory's grace,

And suddenly, Daddy—your voice filled the space.

You found a new way to comfort my fear,

To let me know that your soul is still near.

In radio silence, your love broke through—

A song from the past, still shining true.

Diary Entry

April 20

The radio turned on by itself. I know it sounds crazy, but I was *there.* I didn't touch anything. "You Are My Sunshine" came on and I just cried. That was always our lullaby. It felt like he was there, just for that moment, singing me through the grief.

Chapter Seven

The Whisper at My Shoulder

I was folding laundry in my room, lost in thought about the day, when I felt it.

A breath. A soft rush of air over my right shoulder. I turned quickly—no one was there.

But then I heard it. A whisper. So soft it was barely audible, but it came from behind me. I couldn't make out words, just the feeling: comfort. Peace. Protection.
The kind of energy that only Daddy ever gave me.

I stood there for minutes, still as stone, heart racing but not in fear. I whispered back, "I know you're with me."

That night I slept better than I had in weeks.

Poem – The Silent Whisper

You spoke without sound, a breeze on my skin,

A moment of stillness, where grief had been.

No words were needed, your voice I still knew—

The soul doesn't vanish; it flows right through.

Like wind through branches, you touched my side,

Your love, invisible, still acts as my guide.

Though I can't see you, you're never gone—

Your whisper reminds me: I'm never alone.

Diary Entry

April 27

I felt it. The air on my shoulder, the sound that wasn't really a sound—it was *him*. I've never had that happen before. But now I know I'm being watched over.

I'm learning the spirit speaks in quiet ways. You just have to be still enough to listen.

Chapter Eight

The Scent of His Cologne

I was cleaning out the hallway closet when it hit me—the scent. Not faint. Not imagined. A strong, familiar wave of it.

Daddy's cologne.

It stopped me mid-step. That same earthy, woodsy blend he wore every Sunday morning and after work. I hadn't smelled it in years. I didn't even keep any of his bottles.

I knelt down, breathing it in, eyes closed. No one else was home. No air fresheners. Nothing sprayed. Just scent—and memory.
I whispered, "I miss you," and felt a calm settle in the room. The scent lingered for a minute more before fading gently, like a goodbye hug.

Poem – A Breath of You

No bottle, no breeze, just suddenly there,

A whisper of you that hung in the air.

Cedar and smoke, warm sandalwood trace,

Wrapped me in comfort, your spiritual embrace.

You walked through my grief, unseen but true,

And left your scent as a gift from you.

Though time and dust may claim the years,

Your memory still brings back my tears.

Diary Entry

May 3

Daddy's scent filled the hallway today. It came from nowhere. I didn't open anything. It wasn't in my mind—it was real. I know it.

That smell used to mean safety. I believe it still does. Thank you, Daddy. I needed that today more than you know.

Chapter Nine

The Black Birds in the Yard

It was early morning, the sky overcast and moody. I stepped outside to feed the dog and there they were—six black birds, all sitting quietly in the yard.

Not moving. Not pecking. Just watching me.

Black birds have always held meaning for me. Messengers. Warnings. Blessings in disguise. I watched them for what felt like forever. Then, all at once, four lifted into the air—spiraling up, wings wide like freedom.

The remaining two stayed, grounded, until I whispered, "Thank you for the sign." Then they too flew off—calm, purposeful.

Some people might say it's just birds. But I know better.

Poem – Wings in the Morning

Six stood still in the morning gloom,

Feathers dark like a sacred plume.

No cry, no sound, just knowing eyes,

And then four soared into the skies.

Two remained, then took their flight,

Vanishing into the misty light.

More than birds, more than sky—

They carry the words of those who die.

Diary Entry

May 9

Six black birds came to the yard today. It didn't feel random. I watched them longer than I probably should've, but I was *waiting*.

When they flew off, it felt like a message. A reminder that I'm being watched over... not by birds, but by my father, using them as wings.

Chapter Ten

The Flickering Candle

It was just a small candle on my bedroom shelf—a lavender one I lit only when I needed calm. That night, I lit it while talking to Daddy in my thoughts. I asked for peace. For presence. For a sign.

The flame burned steady at first... then started to flicker, rapidly, almost like it was dancing in rhythm. I closed the window. No breeze. No fan. Nothing moved except that flame.

It pulsed three times—then stilled.

I remembered something Daddy used to say: "If the light's still burning, I'm not far." It hit me like a warm blanket. I knew that was him.

The candle kept glowing quietly beside me for the rest of the night.

Poem – A Flame That Speaks

No wind, no sound, but still you stirred,

A flickering flame, like a whispered word.

It blinked once, then twice, and then one more—

Three little taps from the spirit door.

You burn without match, you glow with grace,

A quiet reminder, a sacred place.

I speak to the flame and know deep inside,

My father's love has never died.

Diary Entry

May 14

The candle flickered in such a strange way tonight. I watched it pulse three times after I asked for a sign. It wasn't normal. The windows were closed. It felt *intelligent,* like it answered me.

I really believe Daddy is using whatever he can to reach me.

Chapter Eleven

The Music Box That Played Itself

The old music box had been tucked away in my dresser for years. Daddy gave it to me when I was a child—a little ballerina spun inside it when you wound the key. But I hadn't touched it in ages. The key had broken long ago.

I was sitting on my bed one quiet afternoon when I heard it: the delicate, haunting melody of that very music box.

I turned slowly, goosebumps rising. The box was closed. The lid hadn't moved. But the song kept playing—softly, clearly, for nearly thirty seconds.

I didn't cry right away. I just listened, knowing it was a sound only I was meant to hear. And when the music faded, I whispered, "Thanks for visiting, Daddy."

Poem – Ballerina's Waltz

Dusty box, forgotten tune,

A song that danced across the room.

No hand had turned your tiny key,

But there you were, playing for me.

Your melody curled around my ears,

Stirring joy and stirring tears.

Not broken—just waiting to be heard,

You spoke again without a word.

Diary Entry

May 18

I still don't understand how the music box played today. It's been broken for years. I never fixed it. But somehow, the music came through, like a memory waking up.
It was so gentle, so personal... like Daddy used it to tell me he's still close. I'm going to leave it on the shelf now, in case he ever plays it again.

Chapter Twelve

The Numbers on the Clock

I never used to believe in "angel numbers." Repeating patterns, divine timing—I always thought it was just coincidence. But lately, the clock keeps catching my eye.

8:58.

Each time, it's when I'm thinking about Daddy—or when I'm struggling the most. The pattern became too consistent to ignore.

One night, I saw 8:58 flash on my phone just as I was whispering, *"I wish you were here."*

I looked it up: "858" is the number of reassurance, of being on the right path, of divine protection.

Tears welled in my eyes. Daddy wasn't just reminding me of his presence—he was reminding me to trust the journey.

Poem – Repeating Signs

Digits glowing, quiet light,

Patterns forming late at night.

Each set of numbers, bold and true,

Whispers softly, "I'm with you."

Not math, not chance, not random grace,

But love that finds the time and place.

On every clock, in every line—

You show me how our souls align.

Diary Entry

May 25

It's not random anymore. These numbers keep showing up at just the right moments. Always when I'm praying or feeling his absence most.

I think Daddy is using the clocks now—divine timing to say: "Keep going. You're not alone."

Chapter Thirteen

The Shadow in the Mirror

It happened just before dawn.

I was brushing my hair in the bathroom, half-asleep, when something shifted in the mirror. I paused. It wasn't me—it was behind me. A soft silhouette, just for a second. No fear, no chill. Just presence.

I turned around quickly. No one there.

But I *felt* it. A warmth behind me. A knowing. The kind you don't forget.

When I looked back at the mirror, I whispered, "Hi, Daddy," and something inside me calmed. No panic. No confusion. Just peace.

Not all reflections show our own face. Sometimes, they reveal who's watching over us.

Poem – Behind the Glass

A shimmer moved where light should stay,

A flicker passed and slipped away.

No form, no frame, no words to hear—

Just love reflected, standing near.

A guardian soul, a father's grace,

Appearing soft in mirror's face.

In silence, still, I understood—

You showed me signs the way you could.

Diary Entry

May 29

I know what I saw. It was only a second, but the mirror caught it—something more than light. And I didn't feel scared. I felt... accompanied. I think Daddy wanted to remind me he's standing right behind me.

Even now.

Chapter Fourteen

The Message in the Wind

It was one of those still summer afternoons—no movement in the trees, not even the hum of insects. I was sitting on the porch, missing him deeply, when I asked out loud: "Do you still hear me?"

That's when it came—a sudden breeze, just enough to lift the pages of my notebook and rustle the wind chimes Daddy had hung years ago.

They hadn't made a sound in weeks.

The breeze passed gently across my face like a kiss, and the chimes sang out a soft, sweet melody.

It wasn't just weather. It was an answer. I smiled and whispered, "I hear you too."

Poem – Carried on Air

No storm had stirred, no breath had blown,

Yet winds arrived as if they'd known.

A kiss of air, a chime's soft ring,

Your voice returned on angel's wing.

The trees stood still, the clouds stayed shy,

Yet something sacred brushed the sky.

And I, in silence, deeply knew—

That was your soul, just passing through.

Diary Entry

June 2

The wind chimes played today, and I swear it was timed perfectly. No breeze all day until I spoke to him. Then suddenly, the wind came like an answer.
I feel so comforted knowing that nature listens—because he's speaking through it.

Chapter Fifteen

The Lights at the Cemetery

It was dusk when I visited Daddy's grave again. The sun had just dipped below the trees, and the sky was awash in soft lavender and gray.

As I stood by the headstone, talking to him like I always do, I noticed something unusual—tiny flickers of light dancing around the grave. Not fireflies. Not reflections. Just small orbs of soft white and blue light that shimmered, then disappeared.

I blinked, rubbed my eyes, and still they glowed.

They didn't frighten me. They made me feel surrounded. Protected. I felt sure they were spiritual. Maybe ancestors. Maybe Daddy's spirit lighting the path.

I whispered, "I see you."

Poem – Light Among Stones

Among the stones where shadows sleep,

The sky grew quiet, soft and deep.

Then flickers bloomed in evening air,

As if the stars had gathered there.

No flame, no trick, no earthly spark,

But gentle lights that graced the dark.

A father's love, still shining bright,

Glowing softly into night.

Diary Entry

Tonight I saw lights at the cemetery. Not like anything I've ever seen before. They were peaceful... like glowing reminders that Daddy is still with me.

I know what I saw. And I'm not afraid anymore.

Chapter Sixteen

The Voice in the Quiet Room

It was late. Everyone was asleep. I had just laid down when I heard it—a voice.

It wasn't a dream. I hadn't drifted off yet. It was real, and it was gentle.

It said my name.

Just once. Just clearly enough that I sat up straight, heart pounding—not from fear, but from recognition. Daddy always had a way of saying my name when he needed to get my attention. Not loud. Just... *present.*

I whispered, "I hear you," and felt a wave of calm pass through the room like a tide.

That night, I finally slept without tears.

Poem – In the Stillness, Your Voice

No echo, no echo, no sound to chase,

Yet I heard you clearly, in time and space.

One word, my name, your sacred call—

And in that moment, I felt it all.

The distance vanished, the veil grew thin,

And love poured in from deep within.

No need for more, no need to prove—

Your voice remains where silence moves.

Diary Entry

I heard him. I really did. He said my name, soft as breath, but strong enough to reach my soul. It wasn't imagined. It wasn't fear.

It was comfort. Daddy still knows how to call me home.

Chapter Seventeen

The Butterfly That Waited

I was walking along the trail behind my house, needing space to clear my mind. Grief had hit hard again that morning, unexpected and heavy. I asked Daddy aloud, "If you're with me, show me."

That's when I saw it—a large monarch butterfly, orange and black, landing gently on a branch right beside the path. I stopped walking.
It didn't fly away.

I stood just feet from it, and it stayed—wings still, as if holding space for me. After nearly a minute, it fluttered once, then circled around my head and flew upward into the sky.

Not every butterfly is just a bug. Some carry prayers. Some *are* the answer.

Poem – Wings of Comfort

A flash of orange on morning air,

A silent soul that met me there.

No flutter rushed, no need to flee—

You waited there, just watching me.

Around my heart, your wings did glide,

A father's grace you couldn't hide.

With every flight, you prove it true—

The spirit world still walks me through.

Diary Entry

June 18

That butterfly today wasn't a coincidence. It *waited* for me. It felt like Daddy paused time just to say, "I'm here."

I cried, but not out of sadness. It felt like love in motion.

Chapter Eighteen

The Unexpected Song

I was grocery shopping—just a normal day. Nothing emotional, nothing unusual. Then it happened.

Over the store's speaker system came a song I hadn't heard in over twenty years. Daddy's favorite:

"Take It Easy" by the Eagles.

He used to sing it while driving, always tapping the wheel with that half-smile on his face. I stopped right in the aisle. Frozen. Just listening.

The world kept moving, but I stood still—heart full, eyes welling.

Out of all the songs, at that moment, that one? That was no accident.

Daddy turned a routine trip into a sacred reminder.

Poem – Melody in Aisle Four

Among the shelves of bread and beans,

I heard a tune between the scenes.

It found me there with quiet grace,

And pulled a smile across my face.

Not planned, not staged, just flowing through—

A father's voice in something new.

And though the world still rushed around,

That song made sacred, solid ground.

Diary Entry

June 21

The grocery store played *his* song today. I know most people wouldn't think twice, but I do. Because I asked for reminders—and they keep finding me.
I smiled the rest of the day. That was *his way* of checking in.

Chapter Nineteen

The Gentle Touch Before Dawn

It was early—too early for light. I was half-asleep, turned on my side, when I felt it: a soft pressure on my shoulder. Not sharp. Not heavy. Just... a touch. Like someone resting their hand gently, the way Daddy used to when he'd wake me up as a child.

I didn't move.

Tears formed instantly. I knew it couldn't be a dream—I was awake. Fully present. And the comfort in that moment wrapped around me like a warm blanket on a cold morning.

I didn't need words. I didn't need to see him. That touch said everything.

Poem – A Father's Hand

No door was opened, no voice was heard,

Yet I was calmed without a word.

A hand so light, yet strong and true,

Reached from the veil and rested too.

Not phantom fear, but sacred grace—

I felt your soul in that still place.

And now I know, beyond all doubt,

You touch my life from inside out.

Diary Entry

June 27

I swear I felt him touch my shoulder today. It was exactly like when I was little. Gentle, steady, full of love. I didn't imagine it. I know his presence by heart.

That was Daddy, reminding me I'm still his little girl.

Chapter Twenty

The Final Sign — A Dream of Letting Go

This dream was different.

Daddy and I were sitting on a bench by a river—just the two of us. He looked young, strong, peaceful. We didn't speak for a while. Just listened to the water.
Finally, he turned to me and said, "It's time."

I knew what he meant. Not to forget. Not to move on—but to live fully. To stop carrying the weight of sorrow. To *let go* of grief, and hold on to love.

He smiled. Stood. And walked into the mist beyond the trees.

When I woke up, I felt something shift inside me. Not sadness. Not loss. But peace.

The final sign wasn't goodbye—it was permission to begin again.

Poem – River of Release

We sat in silence, heart to heart,

No need for words to pull apart.

The river moved, and so did time,

And then you gave me one last sign.

"Let go," you said, and though I cried,

You gave me wings so I could glide.

I'm not alone. I never was—

Your love still leads me, just because.

Diary Entry

July 1

Last night, he gave me his final gift—a dream of release. I woke up lighter. Not because I let go of *him*, but because I finally understood.
Grief is love with nowhere to go… until we carry it forward, like light.

Thank you, Daddy. I'll keep looking for the signs. And I'll keep living.

About the Author

Sondra Sampson is a proud Lumbee woman, mother of five, and passionate storyteller with a heart rooted in spiritual connection and ancestral strength.

After the passing of her father, Charles Graham Sampson, she began experiencing a series of powerful signs that inspired this book. Through feathers, whispers, and sacred moments in nature, Sondra discovered that the veil between worlds is thin—and that love continues far beyond the grave.

Signs from the Spirit is her first book—a deeply personal journey of grief, hope, and healing. Written with honesty and soul, it invites readers to recognize the sacred messages in their own lives.

Sondra lives in North Carolina with her family and loyal dogs & cats. She honors her father daily by listening for the signs and helping others trust in their own spiritual paths.

Conclusion

The Signs Will Continue

As you turn this final page, I hope you feel what I've felt through every chapter—

That love doesn't disappear.

That grief is sacred.

And that spirit speaks, if you're willing to listen.

These signs were never about grand miracles. They were quiet moments—soft reminders—that my father's love hadn't ended, only transformed. A feather on the windshield. A song in a grocery aisle. A whisper in the dark. They were pieces of proof that the veil between this world and the next is thinner than we think.

I know now that I was never alone—not even on the hardest nights. And neither are you.

This book is more than a tribute to my daddy. It's an invitation for you to start your own conversation with the spirit world. Talk to your loved ones who've passed. Ask them to show you they're near. Be still. Be open. Then watch what unfolds.

The signs will come. Not always when or how you expect—but they *will* come.

Because love never gives up on us. Not even in death.

If this book has reached your heart, then his spirit has touched yours too.

And for that, I say...

Thank you, Daddy. Keep sending the signs. I'm still listening.

Epilogue

Still Watching, Still Guiding

Time moves on, but some moments never leave us.

Since writing these pages, the signs haven't stopped. In fact, they've deepened. A black bird landing near me on days I feel weak. A dream that arrives when I need reassurance most. The scent of sawdust or cologne where there should be none.

I've come to understand that when someone we love crosses over, they don't vanish—they become woven into the very fabric of our lives. They become the song that plays at just the right moment. The feather that falls without wind. The feeling of peace when it shouldn't be possible.

Daddy still shows up.

Not just in symbols, but in strength. In courage. In the ability to wake up on hard days and keep going.

If you've felt something while reading these pages—something warm, familiar, or deeply personal—then maybe a spirit was sitting beside you, too.

This story was mine, but it now belongs to you, to anyone longing for connection after loss. I hope it reminds you to trust your heart, honor your intuition, and never doubt the power of unseen love.

And when you see your own sign—no matter how small—pause.

Breathe.

And say,

"I see you. Thank you."

Afterword

For Anyone Still Waiting for a Sign

If you're holding this book and still wondering if the signs are real, this part is for you.

I know what it feels like to wait—to cry out in grief, to search the sky, to beg for something, *anything*, that proves your loved one is still near. I was there. I've lived it. And here's what I've learned:

The signs don't always come when we ask.

They come when our hearts are ready to receive them.

Sometimes they're soft—a dream, a song, a feeling you can't explain. Other times, they're so strong, they stop you in your tracks. Either way, they are *real*. I've felt them. I've lived them. I've written them down so you could see for yourself.

If no one else has told you this yet, let me be the one to say it:

Your grief is valid.

Your love still lives.

And your person—your parent, your child, your partner, your friend—they are still with you.

This book is proof that signs are everywhere. You just have to slow down, open your heart, and believe they are meant for *you*.

You are not alone.

I pray that after reading *Signs from the Spirit*, you begin to look at the world differently. With more wonder. With more hope. With more trust that your loved one is just a whisper away.

When the next sign comes—and it *will*—smile. They've been waiting for you to notice.

www.ingramcontent.com/pod-product-compliance
Lightning Source LLC
Chambersburg PA
CBHW061715120626
46550CB00003B/1234